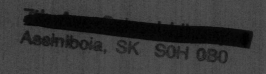

WITHDRAWN

GRAMMAR
BASICS

ADJECTIVES
KATE RIGGS

CREATIVE ♣ EDUCATION

Published by Creative Education P.O. Box 227, Mankato, Minnesota 56002
Creative Education is an imprint of The Creative Company www.thecreativecompany.us

Design and production by Liddy Walseth Art direction by Rita Marshall
Printed in the United States of America

Photographs by Corbis (Heide Benser), Getty Images (Laurence Dutton, Tim Flach, Gone Wild,
Catherine Ledner, Martin Rogers, Kevin Summers, Gandee Vasan), iStockphoto (Andrew Howe,
Eric Isselée, Maria Itina, Angelika Schwarz, sumnersgraphicsinc, Tomasz Zachariasz)

Illustrations pp. 20–21 copyright © 2007 Etienne Delessert

Library of Congress Cataloging-in-Publication Data
Riggs, Kate.
Adjectives / by Kate Riggs.
p. cm. — (Grammar basics)
Summary: A simple overview of adjectives—the words that describe nouns—including their uses in
sentences, their common and proper types, and how to spot articles and different forms.
Includes index.
ISBN 978-1-60818-236-7
1. English language—Adjective—Juvenile literature. I. Title.
PE1241.R56 2012
428.2—dc23   2011050850

First Edition
2 4 6 8 9 7 5 3 1

TABLE OF CONTENTS

INTRODUCTION

What kind of school do you go to? Is it an *elementary* school? How many classmates do you have? Are there about *thirty* students? Which grade are you in? Are you in the *first*, *second*, or *third* grade? Maybe you're not in *any* of those grades!

WHAT ARE ADJECTIVES?

The *big* dog looks down at the *little* dog.

Adjectives are words that explain *what kind*, *how many*, or *which*. They tell these things about other words called nouns. Nouns are people, places, and things. Adjectives usually come before nouns in a **sentence**.

ADJECTIVES IN USE

The *pretty* butterfly spread its *dark* wings.

Every sentence has at least one noun. It also has at least one **verb**. But not every sentence needs an adjective. When you want to tell more about nouns in a sentence, you use adjectives.

TYPES OF ADJECTIVES

The *brown* horse kicked its legs.

There are **common adjectives** and **proper adjectives**. Most adjectives are common: a *blue* lake, a *dirty* shirt, a *broken* arm. Proper adjectives tell about certain people, places, and things.

Best friends snuggled on the couch.

PROPER BEHAVIOR

Proper adjectives always start with a big letter called a capital. Can you find the proper adjective in the sentence below?

Peter found a German coin on the floor.

13

ARTICLE POINTERS

The alligator looked for its *next* meal.

Another kind of adjective is called an article. An article usually comes before a common or proper adjective or noun. *A*, *an*, and *the* are articles. Articles point to the nouns in a sentence. They tell us if the noun is specific (*the* alligator). They also tell us if it is not (*an* alligator).

FROM VERB
TO ADJECTIVE

Sometimes an adjective is made out of a verb. When you add the ending *–ing* to a verb such as *laugh*, you get "laughing."

The laughing girl skipped down the sidewalk.

Laughing tells us *what kind* of girl is skipping, so it's an adjective. *Skipped* is the only verb.

Two friends are better than one.

IT'S ALL IN THE ENDING

Adjectives can end in many ways. When they end in *–er* or *–est*, they could be comparing two or more nouns. A *tall* boy can

Some ducks are *taller* than other ducks.

become *taller* than other boys. He could even be the *tallest* boy you know!

LOOK OUT
FOR ADJECTIVES!

To find an adjective, first look for the noun. Is there another word that tells more about the noun? If you can answer *what kind*, *how many*, or *which*, then you know the word is an adjective!

GRAMMAR GAME TIME

Have you ever done a Mad Lib? This is a story that lets you fill in the blanks with your own words. Use what you know about adjectives to do the Mad Lib on the next page. Be sure to write your adjective and article choices on another sheet of paper!

Once upon ___ (article) time, there was a

_____ (adjective: *what kind*) princess. She

had _____ (adjective: *what kind*) hair. She lived

next to _____ (proper adjective: *which*) Lake.

One day, a _____ (adjective: *what kind*) knight

came to see her. He said, "_____ (adjective:

what kind) princess, I want to marry you!" The

_____ (adjective from a verb: ending in *–ing*)

princess said, "I accept!" The _____ (adjective:

how many) people lived happily ever after.

_____ (article) End

grammar word bank

common adjectives—non-capitalized words that tell more about nouns
proper adjectives—capitalized words that tell more about nouns
sentence—a group of words that has a noun as the subject and a verb
verb—an action or a state of being word; state of being words include *am*, *is*, *are*, *was*, and *were*

read more

Fleming, Maria. *Grammar Tales: The Bug Book*. New York: Scholastic, 2004.

Heller, Ruth. *Many Luscious Lollipops: A Book about Adjectives*. New York: Grosset & Dunlap, 1989.

web sites

Grammar Blast
http://www.eduplace.com/kids/hme/k_5/grammar/
Test your adjective knowledge by taking the quiz at your grade level.

Grammar Ninja
http://www.kwarp.com/portfolio/grammarninja.html
Skilled ninjas can find the adjectives, nouns, and verbs in each sentence.

index